School District 64
164 S. Prospect
Park Ridge, IL 60068

What Are Rules and Laws?

by Jennifer Boothroyd

Lerner Publications ◆ Minneapolis

The images in this book are used with the permission of: © iStockphoto.com/onairjiw, p. 4; © iStockphoto.com/skynesher, p. 5; © Bob Daemmrich/Alamy, p. 6; © Ilfede/Dreamstime.com, p. 7; © Dragonimages/Dreamstime.com, p. 8; © Mirage1/Dreamstime.com, p. 9; © Photographerlondon/ Dreamstime.com, p. 10; © Jean Glueck/F1 ONLINE/SuperStock, p. 11; Official White House Photo by Pete Souza, p. 12; © Steven Frame/Dreamstime.com, p. 13; © brt PHOTO/Alamy, p. 14; © iStockphoto.com/kali9, p. 15; © iStockphoto.com/benkrut, p. 16; © UpperCut Images/Getty Images, p. 17; © Stockbyte, p. 18; © iStockphoto.com/magnetcreative (hallway), p. 18; Jim West imageBROKER/Newscom, p. 19; © iStockphoto.com/lisafx, p. 20; © iStockphoto.com/ftwitty, p. 21.

Front cover: © iStockphoto.com/CEFutcher.

Main body text set in ITC Avant Garde Gothic Std Medium 21/25.
Typeface provided by Adobe Systems.

Lerner Publications Company
A division of Lerner Publishing Group, Inc.
241 First Avenue North
Minneapolis, MN 55401 USA

For reading levels and more information, look up this title at www.lernerbooks.com.

Library of Congress Cataloging-in-Publication Data

Boothroyd, Jennifer, 1972–
    What are rules and laws? / by Jennifer Boothroyd.
        pages cm. — (First step nonfiction)
    Includes index.
    ISBN 978-1-4677-8572-3 (lb : alk. paper) — ISBN 978-1-4677-8617-1 (pb: alk. paper) —
ISBN 978-1-4677-8618-8 (eb pdf)
        1. Law—Juvenile literature. 2. Social norms—Juvenile literature. I. Title.
K246.B66 2015
340—dc23   2014041106

Manufactured in the United States of America
1 – CG – 7/15/15

Table of Contents

NO LITTERING

Rules tell us what we may or may not do.

4

I follow rules in my home.

I follow rules at school.

I stay on
the path.

I follow rules in my
neighborhood.

7

Rules help protect me.

Rules are made to solve problems.

I wait for my turn.

Rules help me be fair to others.

I wear my helmet.

Rules help keep everyone safe.

Making Rules and Laws

Government leaders make some rules.

These rules are called **laws**.

People work together to
make laws.

Families talk about rules.

Making laws is a little like making rules in a family.

Each state and country
has laws.

Older kids may be allowed to use knives.

Rules and laws can change.

Breaking Rules and Laws

This girl ran in the hall.
She broke a rule.

She will be the last one out for recess.

Her teacher gave her a **consequence**.

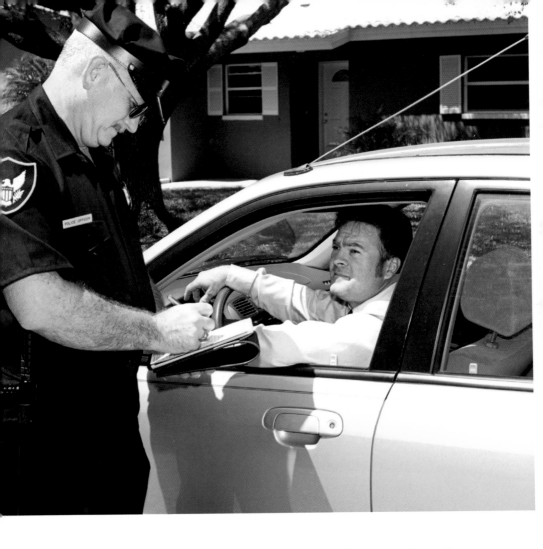

This driver drove too fast.
He broke a law.

The driver will pay a fine.

The police officer gave him a consequence.

It is important for everyone
to follow rules and laws.

Glossary

consequence – the result of an action

government – the people in charge of a city, a state, or a country

laws – rules made by government leaders

rules – words that state what you are allowed or not allowed to do

Index